MW01148598

Watch It Grow

Watch an Apple Grow

by Kirsten Chang

Bullfrog Books

Ideas for Parents and Teachers

Bullfrog Books let children practice reading informational text at the earliest reading levels. Repetition, familiar words, and photo labels support early readers.

Before Reading

- Discuss the cover photo. What does it tell them?

- Look at the picture glossary together. Read and discuss the words.

Read the Book

- "Walk" through the book and look at the photos. Let the child ask questions. Point out the photo labels.

- Read the book to the child, or have him or her read independently.

After Reading

- Prompt the child to think more. Ask: Do you like to eat apples? Can you explain how they grow?

Bullfrog Books are published by Jump!
5357 Penn Avenue South
Minneapolis, MN 55419
www.jumplibrary.com

Library of Congress Cataloging-in-Publication Data

Names: Chang, Kirsten, author.
Title: Watch an apple grow / by Kirsten Chang.
Description: Minneapolis, MN: Jump!, Inc., [2019]
Series: Watch it grow | Audience: Age 5–8.
Audience: K to Grade 3. | Includes index.
Identifiers: LCCN 2018022820 (print)
LCCN 2018024722 (ebook)
ISBN 9781641282697 (ebook)
ISBN 9781641282673 (hardcover: alk. paper)
ISBN 9781641282680 (paperback)
Subjects: LCSH: Apples—Growth—Juvenile literature.
Classification: LCC SB363 (ebook)
LCC SB363 .C43 2019 (print) | DDC 634/.11—dc23
LC record available at https://lccn.loc.gov/2018022820

Editor: Jenna Trnka
Designer: Michelle Sonnek

Photo Credits: Ratikova/iStock, cover; Nadezhda Nesterova/Shutterstock, 1; Roman Samokhin/Shutterstock, 3; Andy Dean Photography/Shutterstock, 4 (boy); Lee jeong-jin/Shutterstock, 4 (background); Billion Photos/Shutterstock, 5; Markus Mainka/Shutterstock, 6–7, 22t; amenic181/Shutterstock, 8; Valentina Razumova/Shutterstock, 9, 23tr, 23bl; TACrafts/iStock, 10–11, 22mr, 23br; J. Marijs/Shutterstock, 12–13, 22br; Natali Glado/Shutterstock, 14–15, 22bl, 23tl; SviatlouSS/Shutterstock, 16–17, 23tr; hans.slegers/Shutterstock, 18; Sari ONeal/Shutterstock, 19; hanapon1002/iStock, 20–21, 22ml; moonlightbgd/Shutterstock, 22ml; Maks Narodenko/Shutterstock, 24.

Printed in the United States of America at Corporate Graphics in North Mankato, Minnesota.

Table of Contents

Fruit Trees

An apple is a tasty snack. Yum!

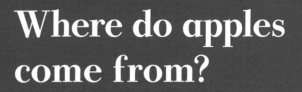

Where do apples come from?

seed

An apple grows
from a seed.

The seed is small.

The seed is planted in the ground.

It needs water.

leaf

stem

roots

It grows roots.
What else?
A stem
and leaves.

It is an apple
tree plant!

The leaves need sunlight.
The plant grows bigger.
It becomes a sapling.

sapling

The sapling grows into a tree.

It takes years.

Flowers bloom in the spring.

They are pink and white.

pollen

Bees fly from
flower to flower.

They spread pollen
from the flowers.

This makes the
fruit grow.

Apples grow big and round.

Different trees grow different apples.

Some are red.

Some are green.

In the fall, they are ready to pick.

We pick them by hand.

Life Cycle of an Apple

How does an apple grow?

seed

sapling

apples

apple tree

flowers

22

Picture Glossary

bloom
To produce flowers.

pollen
Tiny yellow grains that
cause plants to form seeds.

roots
Parts of a plant that grow
underground and get water
and food from the soil.

sapling
A young tree.

Index

To Learn More

Learning more is as easy as 1, 2, 3.

1) Go to www.factsurfer.com

2) Enter "watchanapplegrow" into the search box.

3) Click the "Surf" button to see a list of websites.

With factsurfer.com, finding more information is just a click away.